GRIEF, *Giggles* & GRACE

A LIGHTHEARTED GUIDE TO NAVIGATING THE LOSS OF A LOVED ONE

Tamiko Drummond

Grief, Giggles & Grace

Publisher © 2025

This book is a work of nonfiction based on personal experience. Names and identifying details have been changed to protect privacy where applicable. The author does not offer medical, legal, or psychological advice.

Cover Design & Interior Layout: Tamiko Drummond
Printed in the United States of America
First Edition: 2025
ISBN: 978-1-954071-15-5
Also available in eBook format.

DEDICATION

For everyone who has ever faced the loss of a loved one—may these pages offer you comfort, hope, and light. Grief touches us all in different ways and this book is written for you.

PREFACE

This book was born from the universal experience of grief—silent mornings, unexpected tears, laughter that surprises you, and love that never fades. I didn't write this because I have all the answers. I wrote it because I know what it's like to live with loss and to wonder if the ache will ever ease.

Throughout these pages, I share glimpses of my own story, but this is not just about me. This is about you. Your grief may come from losing a parent, a child, a spouse, a sibling, an aunt, an uncle, or a dear friend. Wherever your loss comes from, these pages are a place for you to breathe, reflect, and remember.

If you're holding this book, know this: you're not alone. My hope is that these words hold you gently, bring laughter when you least expect it, and remind you that grief and grace can coexist—even when it feels impossible.

TABLE OF CONTENTS

PART 1:

Understanding Grief

CHAPTER 1:
What is Grief, Really?

I once heard someone describe grief as an invisible backpack. You don't get to put it down. You just get better at carrying it.

That metaphor stopped me in my tracks because it captured what all those well-meaning platitudes miss. People love to say *"grief gets better with time"* or *"time heals all wounds."* That's cute, and I appreciate the sentiment, but please miss me with all of that.

What actually happens is you get stronger. Wiser. More accepting of the mess. Sometimes—when you're ready—you learn to dance with the waves instead of drowning in them.

Here's what I wish someone had told me: Grief is not a straight line. It's more like a scribble—a messy, unpredictable emotional tornado that might include sobbing while cooking in the kitchen or laughing over an old voicemail.

That's completely normal.

When Grief Finds You

For me, grief didn't announce itself all at once. I was pushing through, minding my business—still serving at church and showing up for work—when the waves trickled in. First came the immediate shock of watching my mom take her last breath: the stillness, the surreal quiet, and then having to immediately shift into logistics mode. Funeral arrangements. The business of death. Making decisions about what she'd wear and how she should look, because the hardest part—the part I didn't think I could handle—was making sure that before everyone else saw her for the final time, she looked exactly the way I knew she'd want to be remembered.

I thought I was handling it well. I thought I was strong.

Then the real waves came—months later.
It was the middle of the night, just as the clock struck twelve. A new year. Exactly three months since she passed. Every feeling I'd tucked away came rushing back like a blanket of *"I wish I could just call her one more time."*

I'd be doing the most ordinary things—brushing my teeth, making my tea—and then it would hit me like a freight train: *She's not here. She's not coming back.*

Grief has this sneaky way of showing up when you least expect it. One moment you're functioning perfectly; the next, you're ugly crying in your car because their favorite song came on the radio. Your brain doesn't just miss someone—it replays, reimagines, regrets, and remembers on an endless loop.

For the longest time, I thought something was wrong with me. Why couldn't I just "move on"?

What I discovered changed everything: this experience isn't a character flaw—it's neuroscience.

The Science Behind the Ache

"In humans, it is because your loved one existed that certain neurons fire together and certain proteins are folded in your brain in particular ways... They still physically exist—in the wiring of the neurons of your brain." — Mary-Frances O'Connor, *The Grieving Brain*

Let that sink in for a moment. The person you lost didn't just leave memories. They left actual imprints on your brain. The love you shared literally shaped your neural pathways. Their absence didn't erase that—it just changed how those pathways function.

Grief is your brain's way of learning how to keep loving when presence has become memory. It's learning to love in absence, which is perhaps the most profound form of love there is.

This means when your body physically aches from missing them, when your thoughts loop back to them constantly, when your nervous system jumps at every unexpected reminder—that's not weakness. That's love with nowhere to go, trying to find a new way to exist.

What Grief Actually Looks Like

Here's what no one tells you: Grief doesn't always look like sadness. It can show up as irritability when someone asks how you're doing for the fifteenth time. It can look like brain fog that makes you forget simple words. Bone-deep fatigue that sleep won't fix. Unexpected laughter when you remember their terrible jokes. Complete numbness when you think you should be feeling something. It can even look like overachieving—throwing yourself into work or projects to avoid sitting still with the pain. (Ask me how I know.)

Grief shows up differently for everyone—whether you've lost a parent, spouse, child, sibling, friend, or beloved pet. Every loss carries its own depth and story. What matters isn't comparing one grief to another, but honoring the love behind it all.

The Messy Truth About Grief "Stages"

You've probably heard about the "five stages of grief"— denial, anger, bargaining, depression, and acceptance. Let me tell you what nobody mentions: they're more like a playlist on shuffle than a step-by-step manual.

I lived through all of them, sometimes in one week. Denial hit me at the funeral home when I kept expecting

Mom to walk through the door and tell everyone to stop fussing over her. Anger came when I got mad at her for leaving me to figure out how to adult without her guidance. Bargaining looked like me googling "do cell phones work in heaven" at 2AM, desperately wanting to make some kind of deal with God.

The depression wasn't just sadness—it was the exhaustion that made choosing what to wear feel impossible. And acceptance? That didn't mean "getting over it." It meant learning to carry both the love and the loss without one canceling out the other.

These stages aren't a graduation ceremony. You don't climb them like a ladder and earn a diploma in "Successfully Processed Grief." You might circle back to anger three years later when you hear someone laugh exactly the way they used to. You might even bargain with God on a Wednesday afternoon or you might feel all the stages in a single afternoon.

That's completely normal.

There's no wrong way to grieve. However it shows up for you—messy, unpredictable, or completely different from what you expected—it's real. It's valid. You're not broken. You're just learning to love in a new way.

Carrying Forward

That invisible backpack? You'll learn to adjust the straps. You'll figure out what pockets hold your most treasured memories and which ones need to stay zipped up on the hard days. Some days it will feel heavier than others, and that's okay. Some days you'll barely notice its weight, and that's okay too.

There is no grief without love. That kind of love—the kind that rewires your brain and changes your heart forever—doesn't just disappear. It sits beside you, walks with you, and slowly transforms from a source of pain into a source of strength.

You will carry this love forward, one shaky day at a time. Eventually, you'll discover that the weight you're carrying isn't just grief—it's also grace.

► *Scripture of Comfort*

"Blessed are those who mourn, for they will be comforted." — Matthew 5:4 (NIV)

This is where grief and grace begin to meet—right here, in the honesty of your heart and the comfort of His promise.

✎ *Reflection Prompts*

1. If you had to describe your grief in three words today, what would they be?
2. When do you notice your grief showing up most? (Be honest—this is your safe space.)
3. Which "stage" of grief feels closest to what you're experiencing right now—and how did it show up for you?
4. Write down one thing you miss about your loved one that still makes you smile.

Your Reflections:

____

____

____

____

____

____

____

____

CHAPTER 2:
Trying to Explain Grief to Other People

Picture this: You're standing in a store, minding your own business in the shampoo aisle, when someone from your past life spots you. They get that head-tilted, concerned look and corner you with the question:

"So... how are you doing?"

Now, this person probably has a good heart. But you're standing there, holding back a tidal wave of tears, wondering if "Fine" is a lie or a survival tactic. (Spoiler: it's both.)

Here's the thing about trying to explain grief: it's like trying to explain what it feels like to breathe underwater. You might not drown, but you're never quite breathing the same again either.

The Hall of Fame of Things People Say (That Make You Want to Scream into a Pillow)

Let me paint you a picture of some greatest hits I've collected:

"At least she's not suffering anymore."
What I heard: Your pain doesn't matter because hers is over.

What I wanted to say: True, but that doesn't mean I don't miss her laugh when I'm making her favorite pancakes on Sunday morning.

"She's in a better place."
What I heard: You should be happy about this.
What I wanted to say: Yeah, I am happy that she's in a better place but it doesn't make me miss her any less.

"God doesn't give us more than we can handle."
What I heard: Your grief is part of some divine plan you should accept gracefully.
What I wanted to say: I'd like to formally request a limit review with management.

"At least you had her for X number of years."
What I heard: You should be grateful and stop being sad now.
What I wanted to say: And I would have loved to have 100 more. That's kind of the point.

Here's the uncomfortable truth: most people would rather say something unhelpful than sit with the awkwardness of saying nothing. They're not trying to hurt you—they're trying to make themselves feel better about your pain. It's human nature to want to "fix" what makes us uncomfortable, even when the person in pain isn't asking to be fixed.

So What Do You Actually Say?

After months of awkward encounters, I developed some go-to responses that protected my heart without burning bridges:

When you're barely holding it together:
"I don't know how I'm doing. But I'm here."

When you need space but want to be kind:
"Thank you for checking in. I'm not ready to talk about it today."

When someone offers advice you didn't ask for:
"I appreciate that you care. Right now I just need people to sit with me in this."

When you're worn out from explaining:
Nods graciously and heads home to fall apart in private... (Yes, that's completely valid too.)

My personal favorite for persistent question-askers:
"Grief doesn't have a timeline, and I'm learning that the hard way."

Setting Boundaries, Not Building Walls

This chapter isn't about throwing shade—it's about protecting your heart. You have every right to set boundaries around your grief without feeling guilty about it.

You don't have to perform your grief for anyone. You don't have to translate it into bite-sized pieces so others can digest it comfortably. You don't have to educate every well-meaning person about loss, and you definitely don't have to pretend you're "doing better" to make them feel less awkward.

Your grief belongs to you and the love you shared with the person you lost. Some days you'll have the energy to help others understand. Other days, protecting your peace is the kindest thing you can do—for everyone involved.

The people who truly love you will learn to sit with your sadness without trying to fix it. They'll stop offering solutions and start offering presence. The ones who can't? That's information worth having too.

A Different Kind of Comfort

What I wish someone had told me is this: the right people will find you. The ones who've walked through their own dark valleys will show up with tissues instead of advice. They'll bring you coffee without expecting conversation. They'll text you "thinking of you" on random Tuesdays without expecting a response.

Here's what I learned about those people: I bought a box of thank you cards after the funeral, fully intending to send one to everyone who showed up, brought food, or checked in. That box sat on my kitchen counter for months. Every time I looked at it, I'd think, "I should do that," but I couldn't. I didn't have the words. I didn't have the energy. Honestly? The right people never needed the card. They understood that my silence wasn't ingratitude—it was survival. They kept showing up anyway—not just in the first month, but in the months that followed when everyone else moved on. (*When they text "thinking of you," I respond with a heart or praying hand emoji—small acknowledgments that don't require words I don't have.*)

These people become your grief tribe—the ones who understand that healing isn't linear, that anniversaries are hard, and that love doesn't end just because breathing stopped.

► *Scripture of Grace*

"Even when I walk through the darkest valley, I will not be afraid, for you are close beside me." — Psalm 23:4 (NLT)

Grief is a valley. Not everyone can walk with you through it, and that's okay. But God can. The love you carry doesn't leave—it echoes through every step, reminding you that you're never truly alone.

✎. *Reflection Prompts*

1. What's the worst thing someone has said to you since your loss? (Go ahead, be petty here—this is your safe space.)
2. What's something you wish someone had said or done instead?
3. Write your personal "go-to" response for the next time someone asks how you're doing—one that feels authentic to you, with or without tears.
4. Who in your life has shown up well during your grief? Take a moment to appreciate them.

Your Reflections:

____

____

____

____

____

____

____

CHAPTER 3:
Why Grief Doesn't Have a Deadline

Let me tell you about the most annoying question I got after my mom died: "How are you doing *now*?"

The emphasis on *now* always got me. Like there was some magical expiration date I was supposed to hit. Three months? Six months? A year? When exactly was I supposed to stop missing the person who shaped my entire world?

There's this unspoken social contract that at some point—after you've cried enough, after you've posted the tribute photos, after people stop bringing casseroles—you'll "be okay again." You'll stop crying at random moments. You'll start moving forward like a good little griever. You'll get back to "normal."

But here's what I wish someone had told me: There is no normal after your loved one dies. There's only your new way of living—and loving—from this side of heaven.

Grief is Not a Broken Arm

People love timelines. Broken arm? Six to eight weeks in a cast. Surgery? Two weeks recovery. Grief? Well, that's where everyone gets uncomfortably quiet because grief doesn't follow medical charts or healing schedules.

Grief is not a broken bone that mends on schedule. It's more like learning to live with a completely different heartbeat. Some days you'll feel like you're soaring. Other days you'll crumble when you find a handwritten note in one of their books.

I remember being "fine" for almost three weeks straight—going to work, laughing with friends, feeling like maybe I was getting the hang of this whole "moving forward" thing. Then one Thursday morning, I heard a ringtone on TV that was exactly like the one my mom used to have, and I completely fell apart—sobbing in my home office just minutes before I had to show up on a Zoom call with a smile on my face.

That's when I realized: grief doesn't do calendars.

When Grief Shows Up Uninvited

Your grief will show up uninvited to places you least expect it. It'll crash your Saturday afternoon because someone wore their favorite color. It'll ambush you at weddings when they play "your song." It'll sneak up on you years later in the parking lot at church on Mother's Day, Father's Day, or their birthday.

You might think you've "moved on," whatever that means, and then find yourself sobbing at the DMV because the person at the counter reminded you of something they used to say.

This doesn't mean you're broken or stuck or doing grief "wrong." It means you loved someone deeply, and that kind of love doesn't follow anyone else's timeline. It shouldn't have to.

Let's Stop Measuring Progress by Tears

Here's a wild idea: what if healing isn't measured by how few tears you cry?

Sometimes tears are healing. Sometimes laughter over their terrible jokes is healing. Sometimes cleaning out their closet is a form of healing. Sometimes leaving it exactly the way they left it for another year is also healing.

Sometimes healing looks like finally being able to listen to their favorite song. Sometimes it looks like avoiding it completely. It might even look like talking about them constantly. At other times it'll look like needing space from their memory for a while.

Your grief doesn't need to match anyone else's timeline, and it sure doesn't need to be explained or defended. The people who love you will learn to stop asking "Are you better yet?" and start asking "How can I walk with you today?"

Permission to Take Your Time

What if instead of rushing toward some imaginary finish line, you gave yourself permission to grieve at your own pace?

What if you stopped apologizing for still missing them six months later, or two years later, or twenty years later?

What if you let yourself feel whatever comes up—sadness, anger, relief, guilt, love, all of it—without judgment?

The truth is, you're not trying to "get over" your loved one. You're learning to carry their love with you in a new way. And that kind of transformation doesn't happen on anyone else's schedule. It happens on love's schedule, which has always been beautifully, mysteriously, perfectly imperfect.

► Scripture for the Journey
"He heals the brokenhearted and binds up their wounds." — Psalm 147:3 (NIV)

This journey is not linear, and it's not supposed to be. But healing is happening—quietly, slowly, deeply— even when you can't feel it yet.

✏️ *Reflection Prompts*

1. What "timeline" have you felt pressured to follow in your grief? Where do you think that pressure came from?
2. Describe a moment when you thought you were "okay" and then weren't. What did that moment teach you about grief?
3. If your grief could speak, what would it tell the people who keep asking if you're "better yet"?

Your Reflections:

____

____

____

____

____

____

____

PART 2:

Living With It

CHAPTER 4:
When the World Keeps Going

The cruelest thing about grief isn't the loss itself—it's how the rest of the world just... continues.

Your person dies, and somehow the sun still has the audacity to rise. People still go to work like nothing happened. Amazon still delivers packages. Bills still show up in your mailbox. Somewhere out there, someone is posting "Live, Laugh, Love" content while you're wondering how you're supposed to brush your teeth when your heart just exploded.

Meanwhile, you're sitting on the edge of your bed in yesterday's clothes, trying to remember if you fed the dog, because your brain feels like it's operating on dial-up internet in a high-speed world.

Grief Doesn't Give You PTO

Let's talk about the myth of bereavement leave. You might get three to five days off if you're lucky—barely enough time to plan a funeral, let alone process the fact that someone who was texting you last week will never text you again.

Guess what? Grief doesn't stop just because your calendar says "Back to Work." It doesn't pause because your family needs you to start cooking again. It doesn't take a break because you've "been quiet long enough" and people are starting to worry.

Here's what I learned the hard way: the world might keep spinning at breakneck speed, but you get to move at your own pace. You get to feel. To grieve. To go slow. You don't have to keep up with everyone else's timeline for your healing.

Welcome to Zombie Mode

Can we talk about the fog for a minute? That weird, underwater feeling where everything feels muffled and far away?

After my mom passed, I found myself doing the dishes one night and suddenly realized I'd been standing at the sink for fifteen minutes, just staring at one spoon. No music playing. No tears falling. Just... existing in this strange space between functioning and falling apart.

That's grief, friends. Some days you're surprisingly productive. Some days you're completely frozen. Some days your biggest accomplishment is making it to 8PM so you can go to bed without anyone asking if you're okay.

All of it counts. All of it is part of the process. All of it is perfectly, completely okay.

I used to think something was wrong with me when I couldn't concentrate on simple conversations or forgot words I'd known my whole life. Turns out, grief is exhausting work. Your brain is literally rewiring itself to understand a world without this person in it. Of course you're tired. Of course you need more time.

Permission to Opt Out (Without the Guilt)

So let's make this practical. Here's your official permission slip to:

- Skip the baby shower where everyone will ask how you're doing
- Leave the group chat on read for as long as you need
- Say "no" to the potluck without explaining why
- Sit out of the family gathering without guilt
- Decline the girls' trip you're "definitely not ready for"
- Turn down the wedding invitation that feels too overwhelming

Your emotional capacity is different now, and that's not a character flaw—it's a fact. Honor it the same way you'd honor a physical injury that needed time to heal.

The people who truly love you will understand. The ones who don't? Well, that's information worth having too.

Finding Your New Rhythm

Eventually—and I mean eventually, not on anyone else's timeline—you'll start to find small rhythms that work for your new reality. Maybe it's coffee in their favorite mug every morning. Maybe it's avoiding the grocery store on Sundays because that was your day together. Maybe it's taking a different route to work because the old one holds too many memories right now.

This isn't about "moving on"—it's about learning to move with. With their memory. With your love for them. With the reality that life looks different now, but it can still be beautiful.

▶ *Scripture for the Overwhelmed*

"Come to me, all of you who are weary and carry heavy burdens, and I will give you rest." — Matthew 11:28 (NLT)

You don't have to hustle through your heartbreak. You don't have to perform productivity to prove you're healing. Rest is holy too.

1. What does "zombie mode" look like for you? How can you be gentler with yourself when you're in that space?
2. What's one thing you can opt out of this week to protect your peace?
3. If your grief could make one request of the world around you, what would it be?

Your Reflections:

____

____

____

____

____

____

____

____

____

CHAPTER 5:
Grief at Holidays and Random Tuesdays

Let's talk about how grief has *absolutely no respect* for timing, location, or your carefully planned emotional schedule.

You might be out in public, perfectly fine, minding your own business, when suddenly your grief decides to make an unscheduled appearance. You see someone with their exact hairstyle walking ahead of you, and your breath catches. Someone's laugh sounds just like theirs. Or you turn down an aisle and suddenly you're standing in the exact spot where they used to pause, reading every label like they had all the time in the world. Or someone casually asks, "Do you have kids?" and you want to say, "Yes, but I'm also someone's kid—and they're not here anymore."

Cue the waterworks. Or the tight throat. Or that awkward speed-walk to the bathroom so you can ugly cry behind closed doors like you're some kind of grief celebrity trying to avoid the paparazzi. (*Been there. Multiple times.*)

When Special Days Feel Especially Hard

Whether it's Thanksgiving, Mother's Day, Father's Day, their birthday, or just regular Sunday dinner, there's something so painfully loud about the empty chair at the table. That silence where their voice used to be echoes through every conversation, every toast, every moment when someone would normally turn to ask their opinion.

I learned this at my first Thanksgiving after Mom died. I spent three days cooking all her recipes, thinking maybe if I could get the jerk chicken & oxtails seasoned exactly right, it would feel like she was still there. I set the table with her favorite dishes, even put flowers in the vase she always used.

But when we sat down to eat, all I could focus on was her empty chair. No matter how perfectly I'd recreated her menu, nothing could fill the space where her laughter used to live.

The truth is: **You don't owe anyone a "happy" holiday.** Your grief doesn't clock out because it's December or because everyone else is posting gratitude lists. It's allowed to sit at the table with you, uninvited but undeniably present.

The Sneaky Tuesday Ambush

Just when you think you've braced yourself for the hard days, grief sneaks in on the days you least expect it.

One minute you're folding laundry like a normal person. The next minute, you're sobbing into a sock because it smells like the detergent they always used. One minute you're fine at the grocery store. The next, you're texting your best friend "I can't do this" because you saw their favorite ice cream on sale and remembered how they used to eat it straight from the container while watching the news.

These random ambush moments used to make me feel crazy. Why was I breaking down over a sock? Why did seeing their favorite snack completely undo me?

The randomness isn't a bug in your grief system—it's a feature. It's your heart's way of saying, "Hey, remember how much we loved this person? Remember how they were woven into the most ordinary moments of our life?"

Learning to Ride the Waves

I used to fight these moments. I'd try to talk myself out of crying in public, force myself to "get it together," and feel embarrassed when grief showed up uninvited to my Tuesday afternoon.

Here's what I learned: those waves of grief aren't signs that you're moving backward or "not healing fast enough." They're proof that love is still alive in you.

They're your heart's way of honoring someone who mattered, even when the rest of the world has moved on.

Now when grief crashes over me in unexpected places, I try to let it. If I need to abandon my shopping cart and leave the store, I do that. If I need to take a few deep breaths in the bathroom because someone laughed exactly like they did, I take those breaths.

Your ways of riding these waves will be uniquely yours. Maybe you'll learn to carry tissues everywhere. Maybe you'll master the art of graceful exits. Maybe you'll get comfortable saying, "I'm having a grief moment" to people who care about you.

There's no wrong way to navigate these surprise visits from your heart. There's only your way, and it's enough.

Permission to Feel It All

The next time grief shows up uninvited—at the grocery store, during the holiday meal, on a random Tuesday that was supposed to be easy—remember this: You're not broken. You're not "not over it." You're not doing anything wrong.

You're just a person who loved someone deeply, learning to live in a world where that love has nowhere physical to land. Sometimes, that love needs to spill over in tears, in memories, in moments that catch you completely off guard.

Let it. All of it. The tears, the laughter when you remember something funny they said, the anger that they're missing this moment, the gratitude that they were part of your story at all.

► *Scripture for the Wave*

"You keep track of all my sorrows. You have collected all my tears in your bottle." — Psalm 56:8 (NLT)

Every tear that falls is seen. Every moment of missing them matters. Nothing about your grief is wasted or forgotten.

✎ *Reflection Prompts*

1. Describe a time when grief surprised you in an unexpected place. What triggered it, and how did you handle it?
2. Which holiday or special occasion feels hardest without your loved one? What's one small way you could honor them next time?
3. Write a short letter to your grief as if it were a friend. What would you want it to know about how you're feeling today?

4. What's one "random Tuesday" memory of your
    loved one that still makes you smile?

Your Reflections:

CHAPTER 6:
Losing Them, Finding Me

There's something that happens when someone you love passes away—something no one really prepares you for.

Yes, there's the obvious grief. The heartbreak that knocks the wind out of you. The longing that sits heavy in your chest.

But then there's this other moment, days or weeks or months later, when it hits you like a quiet punch to the gut: *"The one person who loved me unconditionally... is gone."*

Maybe it was the parent who knew your different cries before you could even speak, who could tell something was wrong just by hearing your voice over the phone. Maybe it was the spouse who always left the porch light on until you came home safe. The sibling who remembered every inside joke from childhood. The grandmother who prayed for you daily without you even knowing it. The friend who was there through every season, thick and thin.

Now—they're not here. There's no one checking in "just because." No one calling you by that childhood nickname that always made you roll your eyes but secretly love it. No one who loves you with that deep, instinctive, don't-need-to-explain-myself kind of love.

It's a particular kind of lonely. Even in a room full of people who care about you.

When Your Identity Shifts

When my mom left this world, I didn't just lose her—I lost a part of who I thought I was.

For me, it was no longer being someone's daughter in the way I used to be. For you, it might be a different role entirely—being someone's spouse, someone's best friend, someone's sibling, someone's child. Either way, grief has a way of shifting your entire sense of identity.

Who am I now without that relationship that defined so much of my daily life? Who am I without that steady, unconditional love as my safety net?

I remember looking in the mirror about three months after she died and not recognizing my own reflection. I looked older, sure. I was definitely hurting. But there was something else there—something I couldn't quite name at first.

Maybe you've had your own version of that mirror moment—realizing you weren't the same person you were before your loss. That's what I was seeing.

In that ache, in that space where my mother's voice used to live, something unexpected started happening. I began to find pieces of myself—pieces that had always been there but had been quietly resting under the comfort of knowing she was just a phone call away.

I started speaking up more in meetings, the way she always told me I should. I began protecting my peace more fiercely, like she used to protect hers. I caught myself loving people deeper, hugging them tighter, the way she taught me love should feel. Slowly, I started to see my own strength the same way she had always seen it—as something real, something powerful, something that was mine to claim.

It's the strangest thing about grief: it breaks you wide open, and somehow, in all that breaking, it can lead you back to yourself.

(Though I'll admit, there are still moments when I'm making a big decision and I can practically hear her voice in my head saying, "Baby, you know what you need to do." Thanks, Mom. Even in heaven, you're still right.)

You Are Walking Proof

Here's what I've learned about losing the person who loved you most: You don't "move on" from them. You move *with* them.

Their love doesn't disappear when they do. It lives on in the way you laugh at something they would have found hilarious. In the way you stand up for someone being treated unfairly, because they taught you what justice looks like. In the way you cook their favorite recipe and can almost feel them guiding your hands. In the way you show up for others going through hard times, because you know what it means to need someone.

You are their living legacy. You are proof that they were here, that their love worked, that it changed something in this world for the better.

While it's true that no one will ever love you exactly the way they did—with that specific mix of pride and protection and unconditional acceptance—you carry that love with you in every breath forward. You carry their voice in your head, their values in your heart, their belief in you as fuel for becoming who you're meant to be.

The Person You're Becoming

Sometimes I wonder if my mom can see me now—see the woman I'm becoming partly because of her love and partly because of her absence. Maybe you've had that thought too, wondering if your person is watching, if they'd be proud of who you're becoming through this impossible journey.

Grief doesn't just take something from you. If you let it—and this takes time, so be patient with yourself—it can also give you something. It can show you parts of yourself you didn't know were there. It can teach you that you're more resilient than you imagined. It can reveal that the love you received was so good, so strong, that it keeps working even after the person who gave it to you is gone.

You are not the same person you were before your loss. That's not a tragedy—that's transformation. You are becoming someone who knows the weight of love and loss, someone who understands what really matters, someone who can hold both sorrow and joy without letting either one define you completely.

The person your loved one saw in you? The potential they always believed in? That person is still becoming. They would be so proud of who you're choosing to be.

► *Scripture for the Becoming*

"I am fearfully and wonderfully made." — Psalm 139:14 (NIV)

The love you received helped shape who you are, but your worth was woven into you from the very beginning. You are exactly who you're supposed to be, even in the midst of becoming.

✎ *Reflection Prompts*

1. What part of your identity feels different since your loved one passed? How are you growing into this new version of yourself?
2. What did your loved one always see in you that you're only starting to recognize in yourself now?
3. Write a letter from your loved one to the person you're becoming. What would they say about your journey?
4. How do you see their love still working in your life today?

Your Reflections:

____

____

____

____

____

____

____

____

PART 3:

Laughing Through It

CHAPTER 7:
Things They Said That Still Make Me Laugh

Grief is a strange, wonderful, terrible thing. One minute you're crying in bed wondering how you'll ever feel normal again, and the next minute you're cracking up at something your loved one used to say that still lives rent-free in your head.

This happens because people are funny. Sometimes on purpose, sometimes completely by accident, and sometimes in that *only-they-could-say-it* kind of way that becomes part of your family folklore forever.

For me, that was my mom. Mothers have their own special brand of humor—part wisdom, part sass, part "I brought you into this world" authority that somehow makes everything they say both hilarious and slightly terrifying.

Classic Sayings We Still Repeat

Here are a few gems that *still* get me every time:

"You better fix your face before I fix it for you."
Trust me, I knew exactly what that meant. The fact that I caught myself saying it to my own son years later?

Well, that's when I realized her voice had officially taken up permanent residence in my head.

"You smell like outside."
Listen, I absolutely know what "outside" smells like now, and she was completely right every single time. It's a very specific scent that apparently clings to you after you've been... outside.

"Why is your hand so dry?"
She asked me this even during one of our last visits in the hospital, reaching over to feel my hands like she always did. Now I never leave the house without lotion, because apparently soft hands matter even more when you're carrying someone's legacy forward.

"When it rains, it pours."
I used to not love this phrase, but she was rarely wrong. It was her way of preparing me for the fact that life sometimes dumps everything on you at once. She wasn't being pessimistic—she was being realistic so I wouldn't be caught off guard.

These are mine. Yours may look completely different—but I bet you have your own version of these phrases, sayings, or specific tone-of-voice moments that still echo in your mind like they're standing right there with arms folded and an eyebrow raised. Maybe it wasn't your mom. Maybe it was your dad's terrible puns that made everyone groan, your grandmother's colorful commentary about the neighbors, your spouse's ridiculous observations about everyday life, or your best friend's ability to find humor in absolutely everything.

Whatever the relationship, grief holds onto the sound of their laughter and the memory of their wit. And that's a gift.

Funny Memories That Hit Different Now

There was the time my mom tried to use emojis and accidentally sent me random emojis that made no sense. She also attempted FaceTime but held the phone at forehead level the entire call, giving me a lovely view of her ceiling while she wondered why she couldn't see me.

There was her "church whisper" that was somehow louder than most people's normal speaking voice, and the way she could give me a look that said *everything* without uttering a single word. That look could stop me mid-sentence from across a crowded room.

At the time, I'd pretend to be annoyed or try not to laugh out loud. Now? I'd give anything to hear her whisper-scream one more time or get another one of those looks that said, "Child, you have lost your mind, but I love you anyway."

Maybe your person had their own version of technological struggles, or their own way of making you laugh without even trying. Maybe they had catchphrases that annoyed you then but make you smile now. Maybe they had a way of finding humor in situations where no one else could see anything funny.

These moments matter more than you might realize. They remind you that your loved one was so much more than their role in your life. They weren't just your parent, spouse, sibling, or friend.

They were also your comedian, your source of unexpected wisdom wrapped in humor, your favorite person to laugh with even when you were laughing *at* them.

Laughter Is Not Betrayal

Let's clear something up right now: Laughing after loss doesn't mean you're "over it." It doesn't mean you've forgotten your person or that you're not grieving properly. It doesn't mean you're doing grief wrong.

Laughter is how your body remembers joy. It's how your soul says, "I'm still here, and so is the love we shared." It's proof that their impact on you was about more than just sorrow—it was about the full range of human experience, including the kind of deep belly laughs that made your sides hurt.

Honestly? Your loved one would want to see you laugh. They'd want to know that their words, their quirks, their particular brand of humor is still bringing light into your days. They'd probably be pleased to know they can still make you smile from wherever they are now.

When you laugh at something they said or did, you're not leaving them behind—you're carrying their joy with you. You're letting their sense of humor continue to live and breathe in this world through you.

Keeping Their Voice Alive

Sometimes I catch myself telling people stories about my mom's sayings, and I realize I've become a keeper of her humor. I'm the one who remembers exactly how she said things, the facial expressions that went with certain phrases, the perfect timing she had for her one-liners.

Maybe you've become that person too—the one who can do the voice, who knows all their favorite expressions, who finds yourself quoting them without even thinking about it. That's not just nostalgia. That's love in action. That's their humor living on through you.

Their laughter echoes in yours. Their wit sparkles in the stories you tell. Their ability to find light in dark places becomes part of how you navigate your own difficult days.

Sometimes, when you least expect it, you'll say something in just the way they would have said it, and for a moment, they feel incredibly close. Those moments are gifts—reminders that love and laughter are forever things, even when the person who gave them to you isn't physically here anymore.

► *Scripture of Joy*

"He will yet fill your mouth with laughter and your lips with shouts of joy." — Job 8:21 (NIV)

Grief may change your laughter, but it doesn't erase it. Even Scripture promises joy can return.

✎ *Reflection Prompts*

1. What's one thing your loved one used to say that still makes you laugh? Write it down exactly how they said it, with all their inflection and attitude.
2. What's a funny memory with them that you can't think about without smiling? What made it so special?
3. When was the last time you laughed and felt their presence in that moment? How did it feel to carry their humor forward?

4. What's one of their sayings or expressions that you've found yourself using? How does it feel to keep their voice alive that way?

Your Reflections:

____

____

____

____

____

____

____

____

____

____

CHAPTER 8:
Funny Grief Moments No One Talks About

Grief doesn't just make you smile at old memories. Sometimes it has its own twisted sense of humor—the kind that shows up in the strangest, most awkward moments when you least expect it.

Not because losing someone is funny. It's *absolutely not.* But because grief does something strange to your brain, your body, and your emotions, and sometimes the only logical response is to laugh... or else you'll cry *again.*

When Grief Brain Kicks In

Let me paint you a picture of what "grief brain" actually looks like in real life.

Picture this: the mall parking lot incident—a full hour of my life I'll never get back, spent circling that concrete wasteland like I was tracking a rare species in the wild. Only the species was *my own car*, and apparently I'd forgotten what it looked like, where I'd left it, and which of the mall's approximately seventy-three identical glass entrances I'd walked through.

Every corner of that building wore the same bland face. *Entrance C? Entrance F? The one with the weird potted plants?* They all blurred together into one indistinguishable facade of beige brick and corporate signage.

So I did what any rational person would do: I systematically visited **every. Single. Entrance.** Out one set of doors, power-walk around the parking lot clicking my key fob like I was trying to send a distress signal. *Click-click. Click-click.* Nothing. Back inside, through the food court, out another entrance. *Click-click-click.* Still nothing. Repeat.

By entrance number five, I was no longer walking—I was *performing* a one-woman show of automotive desperation, jabbing that button with increasing aggression while squinting at rows of identical sedans that certainly, were not mine.

That's when the thought crept in: *Did someone steal my car?*

For one brief, paranoid moment, I genuinely considered it, because surely—surely—I would have found it by now if it actually existed in this parking lot. Right?

Finally, defeat won. I called a friend who lived nearby and confessed that I'd somehow misplaced an entire automobile. She arrived, drove me around the perimeter, and then—*then*—had the audacity to ask: "Did you check the upper level?"

The. Upper. Level.

We went up the ramp, and there it sat. Same beige concrete. Same glass doors. Same view of identical parking spaces stretching into infinity. Except now with my car in it, looking smugly unbothered, as if I were the one who'd wandered off.

Turns out, every level of a parking garage looks *exactly the same* when you're not paying attention.

These moments aren't just regular forgetfulness. They're what happens when your brain is using most of its processing power to figure out how to exist in a world without your person, leaving very little left over for things like "remembering where you parked" or "basic problem-solving skills."

Awkward Conversations We've All Had

Just when you think grief brain only affects your actions, you discover it tangles up your words too.

Your mouth stops cooperating with your brain, and suddenly you're saying things that would've made perfect sense in your head but sound completely ridiculous out loud.

Here are real things I've said (or almost said) to well-meaning people:

"She passed away— I mean, she's with the Lord. I mean, she died. Sorry."
It seems that I couldn't decide which euphemism felt right and tried to use all of them at once.

"Yes, I'm okay." (starts crying two seconds later)
The classic grief contradiction. You genuinely believe you're okay until the tears prove otherwise.

"Thank you so much for the... fruit? And is that cheese?"
When someone brings you a casserole—something you desperately need because you've forgotten to eat and can't remember the last time you cooked—but instead of saying "this helps more than you know," your brain decides to narrate the ingredient list.

Maybe you've had your own version of these moments—saying something that made perfect sense to grief-brain-you but left everyone else confused or concerned. It's part of the process, even when it feels embarrassing.

When Laughter Crashes the Breakdown

Sometimes grief throws both tears and laughter at you in the same moment, which creates some of the strangest experiences you'll ever have.

There I was one afternoon, full-on ugly crying on my couch—the kind of crying where you can't catch your breath and your face looks like you've been stung by bees. I started laughing at the thought of what my mom would say if she could see me in that moment: "*Child, you look a mess. Go fix your face and drink some water.*"

It's wild how grief and giggles can occupy the exact same moment without canceling each other out.

One second you're curled in a ball wondering how you'll survive the next hour. The next, you're cracking up because you found a video on your phone of your loved one singing along to their favorite oldies song, giving it their absolute all with zero shame or concern for anyone watching.

These moments feel bizarre when they happen. You almost feel guilty for laughing in the middle of missing them so deeply. But those bursts of unexpected laughter aren't random—they're reminders. They're your heart's way of saying, "Remember? They made you laugh. They'd want you to keep laughing."

Why the Funny Stuff Actually Matters

Those "oops" moments when you can't find your car or accidentally tell the grocery store cashier your life story? The messy, awkward, uncontrollable bursts of laughter that interrupt your crying sessions?

They're not just amusing anecdotes to share later. They're little gifts disguised as chaos. Tiny reminders that you're still here, still human, still capable of finding light even when everything feels dark.

They're proof that your soul hasn't gone completely numb, that even in the deepest mourning, joy can still find a way to sneak in through the cracks. And honestly, those moments of unexpected laughter often feel like your loved one is right there with you, probably laughing *at* you more than with you, if we're being real.

Because that's what people who love you do—they find ways to make you smile even when they can't physically be there to do it.

So when grief brain makes you do something ridiculous, when you find yourself laughing in the middle of crying, when you say something completely awkward to a well-meaning friend—give yourself permission to find the humor in it. Your loved one probably would.

► *Scripture for the Messy Middle*

"A cheerful heart is good medicine, but a broken spirit saps a person's strength." — Proverbs 17:22 (NLT)

Let yourself laugh. It's holy, it's healing, and your loved one would probably be right there laughing with you... or at you. (Let's be honest.)

✎. *Reflection Prompts*

1. What's the weirdest or funniest thing that's happened to you while grieving? How did it make you feel in the moment?
2. Have you experienced laughter interrupting tears lately? What triggered that mix of emotions?
3. Write about a time when "grief brain" made you do something that you can laugh about now.
4. What's something your loved one used to do that you took for granted then—but now makes you smile?

Your Reflections:

____

____

____

CHAPTER 9:
When Memories Are A Mood Swing

Memories don't come with warning labels. They just show up—unannounced, unfiltered, and usually at the *most inconvenient* time.

You might be having a genuinely good day. Sun's out, your playlist is hitting just right, you even put on real pants instead of leggings for the third day in a row. You're feeling almost normal, whatever that means anymore.

Then boom! You open a drawer looking for batteries and find their handwriting on an old birthday card, or your hand brushes against fabric that feels exactly like their favorite sweater, or your phone suggests a memory from three years ago and there they are, smiling at you from the screen.

Suddenly your heart feels like it's sprinting while your face is frozen in that quiet, internal panic of "Oh no, not right now, please not right now..." But grief doesn't check your calendar before it crashes your Friday afternoon.

The Memory Spiral

Here's what nobody tells you about grief memories: the same memory can hit completely differently depending on the day.

That video of them laughing at your terrible joke? Last month it made you smile. Today it might wreck you so completely you have to pull over and cry in a parking lot. Next week? It might make you laugh and cry at the same time, which is its own special kind of emotional chaos.

I remember finding one of my mom's scarves in my coat closet about six months after she passed. I'd worn that coat a hundred times without noticing it there. But that particular Tuesday, when my hand brushed against that soft fabric, I completely lost it. I sat on my closet floor for twenty minutes just holding it, crying because it still smelled faintly like her perfume.

The weird part? Two weeks later, I found another scarf of hers, and instead of crying, I smiled. I wrapped it around my neck and wore it all day like she was giving me a hug. Same loss, same type of memory trigger, completely different emotional reaction.

That's the memory spiral. It doesn't follow logic or timelines or your carefully managed emotional state. It just is.

When Remembering Becomes Missing

There's a particular kind of ache that comes with certain memories—the ones that remind you not just of who they were, but of all the moments you'll never get to share with them.

Remembering feels tender, almost sacred. It's like your heart lights up for a second as you recall their laugh, their favorite saying, the way they made everything feel manageable just by being there.

But missing? Missing feels like a physical weight in your chest that no hug can fix. It's the difference between "I'm so glad we had that moment" and "I would give anything to have one more moment like that."

Sometimes these two experiences crash into each other. You'll laugh remembering something hilarious they said, and then immediately start crying because you'll never hear them say something new again. You're grateful for the memory and devastated by the loss at the exact same time.

I had this happen at a family dinner when someone told a story about something ridiculous my mom did years ago. Everyone was laughing, and I was laughing too, genuinely enjoying the memory. Then, in the middle of that laughter, grief sucker-punched me with the realization that she wasn't there to add her version of the story or laugh along with us.

The table kept laughing. I excused myself to the bathroom and cried. Five minutes later, I came back and finished my dinner. That's what grief does—it crashes over you, you release it wherever you can, then you carry on like nothing happened.

The Physical Weight of Grief

Here's something I wish someone had explained to me earlier: Even when you think you've "carried on," your body remembers. Grief isn't just an emotional experience. It's physical.

That tightness in your chest when a memory hits? That's real. The lump in your throat that makes it hard to speak? That's your body processing loss. The bone-deep exhaustion that hits you for "no reason"? That's what happens when a memory sneaks in and unpacks all the emotional boxes you thought you'd already dealt with.

After my mom died, I started getting tension headaches that my doctor couldn't explain. It wasn't until my therapist asked, "What were you thinking about before the headache started?" that I realized—I'd been trying so hard not to think about certain memories that my body was literally tensing up from the effort.

Our bodies remember grief even when our minds try to move past it. The memories don't just live in your head—they live in your shoulders, your jaw, your stomach, your heart rate.

Surviving the Memory Waves

So what do you do when memories crash over you unexpectedly? Here's what I've learned, though I'm still figuring it out as I go:

Let them come. I know that sounds simple, maybe even impossible when you're trying to hold it together at work or in public. But fighting memories takes more energy than feeling them. When I stopped trying to control when and how I remembered my mom, the memories became less overwhelming.

This means sometimes I sit in the parking lot for ten minutes collecting myself before I can go inside. Sometimes I have to excuse myself from conversations. Sometimes I let myself sit with a memory for as long as it needs, even if that means being late or canceling plans.

Here's something that surprised me: the more I allowed myself to feel the hard memories, the more space I created for the good ones to surface without destroying me.

Now when memories hit, I try to remind myself: "This means she mattered. This means she still lives—in me, in these moments, in the way her love shaped who I am."

Your tears aren't a setback. Your laughter isn't betrayal. Your ability to feel the full spectrum of memories—painful and joyful—is the most human, most beautiful part of this journey.

► *Scripture for the Whirlwind*

"To everything there is a season, and a time for every purpose under heaven... a time to weep and a time to laugh." — Ecclesiastes 3:1, 4 (KJV)

Some days you'll cry at memories. Some days you'll laugh at them. Some days you'll do both within five minutes. That's not confusion—that's healing.

✎ *Reflection Prompts*

1. What memory of your loved one hits you the hardest? Describe it, no matter how painful or beautiful it feels.
2. Is there a memory you've been avoiding because it feels like "too much"? What would it look like to gently revisit it, even for just a moment?

3. Write a letter to your favorite memory. Start with: "You showed up again today, and here's what you brought with you..."
4. Describe a time when a memory made you feel two opposite emotions at once. How did you handle that?

Your Reflections:

____

____

____

____

____

____

____

____

____

____

PART 4:

Healing Forward

CHAPTER 10:
Coping Without Guilt

At some point in your grief journey, something strange happens.

You catch yourself smiling at a joke. You sleep through the night without waking up in tears. You go to brunch with friends and actually enjoy yourself. You dance in your kitchen while making coffee. Someone mentions your loved one's name, and for the first time, you don't immediately cry.

And then it hits you like a freight train: *"Am I allowed to feel okay?"*

That question—that small, guilty whisper in the back of your mind—is one of grief's cruelest tricks. It's cruel because just when you start to feel like you might survive this, guilt shows up to ask if you have permission to keep living.

When Guilt Crashes the Party

I remember the first time I laughed—really, genuinely laughed—after my mom died. I was about four months out, and my friend told the most ridiculous story about her cat getting stuck in a paper bag. I laughed so hard my stomach hurt. The moment I got home and closed the door, I started crying. Not because I was sad in that moment, but because I felt guilty for having enjoyed myself. How could I laugh like that when my mom was gone? What kind of daughter was I, finding joy when she couldn't be here to experience it with me?

The guilt whispered all sorts of toxic things:

- "You shouldn't be laughing already."
- "How can you enjoy this day without them?"
- "Does this mean you're forgetting them?"
- "What would people think if they saw you having fun?"

None of these thoughts were true. But grief guilt doesn't care about truth—it cares about keeping you stuck.

The Truth About Moving Forward

Here's what I had to learn the hard way: Choosing joy doesn't dishonor your loved one. It actually carries their love forward with you.

Think about it. Did your person pour all that love, wisdom, and care into you so you could pause your life forever? Did they teach you to laugh, to dream, to embrace life fully—only for you to stop doing those things when they died?

My mom would've been furious if she'd known I was crying because I'd laughed at a story about a cat. She would've said something like, "Don't you dare stop living because I'm not there. With God, all things are possible—even learning to laugh again."

You are not dishonoring them by living fully. You're honoring everything they invested in you. You're not "moving on" from them—you're moving forward with their love still wrapped around you like armor.

What Grief Guilt Actually Sounds Like

Guilt sneaks into the smallest moments. It shows up when you least expect it, turning perfectly normal experiences into sources of shame:

At a party: "I shouldn't have come. What if someone thinks I'm over it?"

Watching a movie: "They would've loved this. I feel bad enjoying it without them."

Making plans: "How can I be excited about this trip when they'll never take another trip again?"

Feeling happy: "Something feels wrong. Am I forgetting them by feeling good?"

Let me be crystal clear: None of these thoughts make you a bad person. They simply prove you're still loving, still human, still figuring out how to exist in a world that looks completely different now.

Here's what you need to hear: Your loved one didn't love you so you could stop living. They loved you so you could thrive—even after they were gone.

Permission to Hold Both

One of the most important things I've learned is this: You can grieve deeply and still experience joy. These aren't opposites—they're companions on the same journey.

You can cry in the morning and go out for dinner at night. You can miss them desperately and still enjoy making new memories. You can visit their grave and still celebrate your birthday. You can honor their memory and still pursue your dreams.

Grief isn't all or nothing. It's not a switch you flip from "sad" to "happy." It's learning to hold both sorrow and joy in the same heart, sometimes in the same moment.

I still have days when grief hits me hard. I also have days when I feel genuinely happy, when I laugh without guilt, when I make plans with excitement instead of dread. You know what? Both of those realities can exist in the same week, the same day, even the same hour.

That's not betrayal. That's healing.

What They'd Want You to Know

If your loved one could speak to you right now, in that moment when guilt tries to steal your joy, what would they say?

Would they want you to stop laughing? To refuse happiness? To live a smaller, sadder life because they're no longer physically here?

Or would they want you to dance in your kitchen, to take that trip, to fall in love again, to pursue your dreams, to experience every beautiful thing this world has to offer—carrying their love with you as you go?

I'm betting it's the second one.

Your joy doesn't erase their memory. Your healing doesn't mean you've forgotten. Your ability to keep living doesn't diminish how much they mattered.

In fact, every time you choose joy despite the grief, you're proving just how much they meant to you. Because their love was so strong, so foundational, that it taught you how to rise even when everything in you wanted to stay down.

► *Scripture for the Free Heart*

"So if the Son sets you free, you are truly free." — John 8:36 (NLT)

That freedom includes release from guilt—from the pressure to grieve "the right way" or to prove your love through perpetual sadness. In Christ, even your joy is holy.

✎ *Reflection Prompts*

1. Have you felt guilty for smiling, laughing, or moving forward after your loss? What specifically triggered that guilt?
2. What would your loved one actually say to you in that moment of guilt? (Really imagine their voice and what they'd tell you.)
3. How would your loved one cheer you on if they could see you choosing joy today?
4. List three things you've done lately that felt good for your soul. Now write next to each one: "I deserve this."

Your Reflections:

____

____

____

CHAPTER 11:
Ways to Feel Connected to Your Loved One

You don't stop being who you were to your loved one when they pass away.

That bond doesn't vanish—it shifts. It becomes what I like to call *spiritual muscle memory*, stretching across time and space in ways that surprise you when you least expect it.

One of the hardest parts about grief is the silence. The physical space they used to occupy. The voice you can't hear anymore. The touch you can't feel. The energy that filled a room just because they were in it.

But here's what I've discovered: They may be gone from sight, but they're not gone from your story. There are beautiful, meaningful ways to keep that connection alive—not to keep yourself stuck in the past, but to honor how they shaped who you are today.

Creating Meaningful Moments of Remembrance

About six months after my mom died, I started doing something that became my lifeline: I started writing everything down. Not letters to her—just thoughts. Feelings. The overwhelming mess of emotions that had nowhere else to go. Some days it was a sentence. Other days it was pages of trying to make sense of what I was feeling and how to keep moving forward.

After I'd write, I'd pray. Then I'd search for scriptures that spoke to whatever I was wrestling with that day—comfort, hope, strength, peace. Something to hold onto when everything felt unsteady.

That's why this book looks the way it does. The scriptures at the end of each chapter? The reflection prompts? They're not just nice add-ons. They're what actually helped me process my grief. Writing down what I felt, then turning to God's word for clarity and comfort—that combination kept me from drowning.

At first, it was just for me. A way to survive. But the more I wrote, the more I realized other daughters were probably feeling the same things, asking the same questions, wondering if what they were experiencing was normal. I started thinking about writing a book specifically for daughters grieving their mothers.

Then a friend asked me something that changed everything: "Would you consider making it broader—for anyone experiencing loss?"

That made sense because while my grief was about losing my mom, the feelings—the fog, the guilt, the awkward moments, the faith questions—those are universal. Loss is loss, whether it's a parent, spouse, sibling, friend, or anyone who mattered deeply.

So this book became what it is now: a guide for anyone walking through grief who needs to know they're not alone—and needs practical tools (writing + scripture + reflection) to help them process it all.

This book is what kept me going. And I hope it does the same for you.

Beyond processing grief, there are also beautiful ways to create intentional moments where you feel close to your loved one.

Your moments of remembrance don't have to look like mine. They just have to feel true to you and to the relationship you had. Maybe it's wearing their favorite color on hard days. Maybe it's cooking one of their signature dishes, even if you can never quite get it to taste exactly like theirs. Maybe it's playing their music and dancing around your living room like they're watching from heaven and probably laughing at your moves.

The point isn't perfection. The point is connection. There's no right or wrong way to do this—only what feels real to you.

Paying Attention to How They Show Up

Here's something I've learned to watch for: the moments that feel like more than coincidence.

Maybe it's a specific song that comes on at exactly the right time.

Maybe it's a dream that feels too vivid to ignore.

Maybe it's catching a whiff of their perfume or cologne when no one around you is wearing it.

Maybe it's hearing a phrase you know they used to say, spoken by a complete stranger at the exact moment you needed to hear it.

These aren't just random occurrences. They're reminders that the love you shared doesn't disappear—it just finds new ways to reach you.

I'm not saying every coincidence is a sign. But I do believe grief makes us more aware—more open to the gentle ways love keeps finding us.

Pay attention to those moments. They matter.

Honoring Them by Living Boldly

Here's what took me a long time to understand: Every time you take care of yourself, you're honoring them.

Every time you speak up for yourself, laugh out loud, rest when you need to, or say "no" without guilt—you're becoming more of who they taught you to be.

My mom didn't raise me to fade away in her absence. She raised me to rise. To be strong. To take up space. To love deeply and protect my peace fiercely.

So now, when I do those things—when I set a boundary, when I pursue a dream, when I choose joy even though grief is sitting right next to it—I'm not leaving her behind. I'm carrying her forward. I'm living proof that her love worked.

Your loved one didn't teach you everything they taught you just for you to stop using those lessons. They didn't love you so completely just for you to stop living completely.

Every bold move you make, every risk you take, every moment you choose to show up fully for your own life—that's you honoring their legacy. That's their love continuing to do its work in the world.

The Connection That Never Breaks

The truth is, you're connected to your loved one in ways that death can't touch.

In the values they instilled in you. In the way you love others because of how they loved you. In the strength you discover when you think you have none left, only to realize it's the same strength they always saw in you.

You carry them in your laugh, in your choices, in the way you hug people a little tighter now. You carry them in the traditions you keep and the new ones you create. You carry them in the stories you tell and the memories you protect.

Love chases us—even through grief, even through silence, even when faith feels faint. It finds us in shared laughter, in quiet moments of remembrance, in the courage to keep living boldly.

They're physically gone.
But their presence in your life? That's just different now.
And so are you.
And somehow, in ways you're still discovering, you're both still connected.

► *Scripture for Sacred Connection*
"Surely your goodness and unfailing love will pursue me all the days of my life, and I will live in the house of the Lord forever." — Psalm 23:6 (NLT)

✎ *Reflection Prompts*

1. What are some small ways you already feel your loved one's presence during your day?
2. If you were to create one special moment of remembrance in honor of your loved one, what would it look like?
3. Finish this sentence: "I know they're with me when..."
4. What's one bold thing you've done recently that they would be proud of?

Your Reflections:

____

____

____

____

____

____

____

____

CHAPTER 12:
What Helped Me (And Might Help You Too)

Grief doesn't come with an instruction manual.
Trust me—I looked.

When you're in the thick of it—trying to navigate the fog, the silence, the screaming ache in your chest—sometimes you just need a lifeline. Not advice. Not someone telling you what you *should* do. Just... possibilities. Things that worked for someone else who made it through.

So here's my offering:

These are the things, big and small, that kept me afloat when I thought I'd drown. Not all of them will resonate with you, and that's completely fine. Take what helps, leave what doesn't, and know that your grief toolkit will look different from mine—and that's exactly how it should be.

Therapy: The Space to Understand the Journey

I'll be honest: I resisted therapy at first. I thought I could handle it on my own. I thought talking about it would make it hurt more. I thought I was "strong enough" to push through without help.

But eventually, I realized I wasn't looking for someone to fix me or to give me permission to fall apart—I was already doing that on my own.

What I needed was professional insight. I needed to know: *Am I moving through this grief in a healthy way, or am I stuck?*

Therapy gave me something crucial—understanding.

I learned that grief isn't a neat, linear checklist to complete; it's a series of waves that come and go without warning. Knowing that helped me see that what I was experiencing was normal—that hard days didn't mean I was failing or falling backward.

That realization changed everything. I began to see that the work I was already doing—journaling, praying, searching for scripture—wasn't random. It was healing in motion.

If therapy isn't accessible for you—and I know it's expensive and not everyone has insurance that covers it—many communities offer free grief support groups through churches, hospitals, or nonprofits. Sometimes just hearing someone else say, *"I've been exactly where you are,"* makes the unbearable feel slightly more survivable.

Music: The Soundtrack of Survival

Music became my emotional lifeline in ways I didn't expect.

I created two very different playlists: one for when I needed to cry it out, and one for when I needed to remember that joy was still possible.

The crying playlist?
Full-on Adele, Whitney Houston's *"I Will Always Love You,"* and every gospel song about heaven that's ever been written.
On the hardest days, I'd sit in my living room, turn up the volume, and let myself completely break down.
Sometimes sobbing to the right song is exactly what your soul needs.

The joy playlist was different.
It had Fred Hammond reminding me that God was still good.
It had upbeat songs that made me want to dance even when I didn't think I had the energy.
It had my mom's favorite oldies that I didn't fully appreciate as a kid but now made me smile thinking about her singing along.

Some days I listened to both playlists in the same afternoon.
Some days I couldn't handle either one.

Music met me wherever I was—and that flexibility was a gift.

Rest and Small Acts of Care

This one took me the longest to learn: Grief is exhausting. Like, bone-deep, can't-keep-your-eyes-open, feel-like-you-ran-a-marathon-but-you-only-got-out-of-bed exhausting.

I used to feel guilty about needing naps in the middle of the day or going to bed at 8PM. I thought I was being lazy or weak. But grief isn't lazy—it's survival work. Your brain and body are processing the biggest loss you've ever experienced. Of course you're tired.

So I started giving myself permission to rest.
To take naps without apologizing.
To say no to plans because I genuinely didn't have the energy.
To drink water and eat something nourishing even when I didn't feel like it.
To take a walk outside just to remind myself that the world was still spinning.

Every small act of self-care became an act of *grief survival*. Slowly, those small acts started adding up to something that felt like healing.

Books, Podcasts, and Resources That Helped

These aren't substitutes for professional help or community support, but they were lifelines for me when I needed to know I wasn't alone:

Books:

- *It's OK That You're Not OK* by Megan Devine (This one made me feel less crazy)
- *The Grieving Brain* by Mary-Frances O'Connor (Helped me understand the science behind what I was experiencing)

Podcasts:

- *Griefcast* with Cariad Lloyd
- *Terrible, Thanks for Asking*

Of course, *this book—the one you're holding right now.*

I wrote it because I needed it to exist when I was in the deepest part of my grief.

I needed someone to tell me that grief brain was real, that guilt was normal, that faith and doubt could coexist, and that I wasn't failing just because healing felt impossible some days.

I wrote it for the person sitting in a parking lot at 2PM on a Tuesday, trying to remember if they already cried today or if that was yesterday.

For anyone who just snapped at someone for saying "everything happens for a reason" and now feels guilty about it.

For everyone who's been told they're "too sad" or "not sad enough" and started questioning if they're doing grief wrong.

If this book has helped you even a little—if it's made you feel less alone, given you permission to feel what you're feeling, or simply reminded you that you're not broken—then it's doing exactly what it was meant to do.

You're not alone in this, and you're going to make it through.

▶ *Scripture for the Journey*

"The Lord is close to the brokenhearted; he rescues those whose spirits are crushed." — Psalm 34:18 (NLT)

You are not doing this alone, even when it feels like it. Even in the stillness. Even in the ache. Even when you can't feel His presence, He's there.

✎ *Reflection Prompts*

1. What's something that unexpectedly helped you through your grief, even in a small way?

2. If someone you loved just experienced a loss, what wisdom or comfort would you offer them based on what you've learned?
3. Create your own "Grief Toolkit." What's in it—music, people, places, habits, scriptures, books?
4. Who has shown up well for you during your grief? Have you told them how much it mattered?

Your Reflections:

____

____

____

____

____

____

____

____

____

CHAPTER 13:
A Love Letter to the Griever

Hey you,

Yes, you—the one who's still here. Still breathing. Still aching. Still rising even when rising feels impossible.

I don't know how long it's been since your loved one passed.
Maybe it was yesterday, and the shock hasn't worn off yet.
Maybe it was years ago and you're surprised that grief can still knock the wind out of you.
Maybe you're somewhere in between, in that strange space where time feels both endless and meaningless.

But I know this: you loved them, they loved you, and that love didn't end when their heart stopped beating—it just changed form.

Now it lives in your laugh when you remember something funny they said.
It lives in your strength when you do the hard things they taught you how to do.
It lives in the way you hold others gently when they say they're "fine," but you know better because grief taught you to recognize that particular lie.
It lives in the way you look up at the sky on their birthday and whisper, *"I miss you,"* knowing somehow they can hear it.

You're Doing Better Than You Think

I want you to know something: *you're not failing at grief.*
There's no such thing.

There are no trophies for "most composed at the funeral" or "least amount of tears shed." Healing isn't graded on a curve. There's no timeline you're supposed to follow, no checklist of stages to complete before you're allowed to feel okay again.

You're doing brave work simply by waking up each day—by holding space for their memory while also holding space for your own healing. By allowing your heart to break over and over again while still letting light seep in through the cracks.

Some days your biggest accomplishment is getting out of bed.
Some days it's showing up to work and pretending to be functional.
Some days it's allowing yourself to laugh without immediately feeling guilty.
Some days it's just surviving until bedtime.

All of it counts.
All of it matters.
All of it is exactly what you need to be doing right now.

The Connection Remains

Your loved one sees you. I believe that with my whole
heart.

They see you when you cry in the car before going into
the grocery store.
They see you when you wear their favorite color just to
feel close to them.
They see you when you achieve something they
would've celebrated, and your first instinct is still to call
them before remembering you can't.

They see you showing up for your family even when
you're exhausted.
They see you setting boundaries you never would've set
before, because grief taught you that protecting your
peace isn't selfish—it's necessary.
They see you taking risks they always knew you were
capable of.

I don't pretend to know exactly how heaven works. But
I believe the love that connects us doesn't stop at the
edge of eternity. Whether they're cheering from
heaven's balcony or their love simply lives through us,
that connection remains unbroken. And I believe they're
proud of you.

Not because you've "moved on" or "gotten over it"—
those phrases don't even make sense when you love

someone the way you loved them—but because you're still here. Still choosing to live fully even though a piece of your heart left when they did. Still finding ways to laugh, to love, to hope, to dream.

That takes courage they always knew you had.

You Are Their Living Legacy

Here's what grief has taught me:
You carry your loved one with you in ways that death can't touch—but you also carry forward what they would've wanted for you.

They would want you to keep becoming.
To build the life they once prayed you'd have.
To shine in the places they dreamed of standing beside you.
To keep loving deeply, laughing loudly, and showing up bravely for the life still unfolding ahead of you.

You are their continuation—the living proof that their love changed something lasting in this world.
Every time you choose kindness, you honor them.
Every time you stand up for yourself, you honor them.
Every time you pursue a dream, protect your peace, love deeply, or laugh until your stomach hurts—you honor the love they poured into you.

They're not gone. They're just different now.
They live through you—in the choices you make and
the person you're becoming, shaped both by their love
and by their absence.

Keep Going

So here's what I want to tell you, griever to griever,
heart to heart:

Keep going—even on the days when going feels
impossible.
Keep laughing—even when guilt tries to steal your joy.
Keep loving—even though love now carries the weight
of loss.
Keep honoring them by living boldly, fully,
authentically—the way they always wanted you to.

Your grief is holy ground.
Your healing is a testament.
The love you shared? It's eternal, unbreakable, stronger
than death itself.

They would want you to keep living—not *despite* the
grief, but *with* it.
Carrying both their memory and your own future,
holding both sorrow and joy, being both broken and
whole at the same time. That's okay. It's part of the
journey.

I still catch myself reaching for the phone to call my mom on days I need to celebrate something small. Maybe I always will.
I've learned that healing isn't forgetting—it's learning how to carry their love differently.

You're doing better than you think.
You're stronger than you know.
You are never, ever alone in this.

► *Scripture for the Road Ahead*
"He will wipe every tear from their eyes, and there will be no more death or sorrow or crying or pain." — Revelation 21:4 (NLT)

Until that day comes—may you carry their love like armor and walk forward with grace.

✎ *Final Reflection:*

What would you tell yourself on your hardest grief day? Write it now, for you—and for the next soul who might need your words someday.

CHAPTER 14:
Closing Reflections & Notes

What's Next in Your Healing?

You've walked through stories, scriptures, and prompts, and now you've arrived here—this open space.
But your journey doesn't end with the last page of a book.
Healing doesn't close like a chapter; it unfolds—slowly, quietly—in your everyday moments.

Think of this space as an invitation.
A place for your tears, your laughter, your prayers, your memories, and your growth. A place that belongs fully to you.

Use this space for:

- Free journaling
- Writing down your thoughts, feelings, and memories
- Creating your own prayers or affirmations
- Noting important dates, memories, or quotes you want to hold close

✎ **Journal Prompts to Revisit Over Time:**

1. What does "healing" mean to you now, compared to when you first started this journey?
2. What do you want to carry forward from your loved one's legacy?
3. What message would you give to someone who's just now feeling the weight of their grief?

These pages are yours now.

May they hold your tears and your laughter.

May they hold your prayers and your peace.

May they remind you that even here—between grief, giggles, and grace—you are still healing, still becoming, and still deeply loved.

Your Reflections:

____

____

____

____

____

From My Heart to Yours

This book wasn't just written *for* you—it was written *with* you and your journey in mind.

With every chapter, I wanted you to feel seen. Held. Understood.

I wanted you to know: **You are not alone.**

Your grief is sacred.

Your healing is holy.

The one you love? They're with you. Every single step.

With grief, giggles, and with grace,

—Tamiko

ABOUT THE AUTHOR

Tamiko Drummond is a multifaceted speaker, facilitator, and strategic consultant whose work spans leadership development, branding, and guiding people through life's most challenging transitions. She is the CEO of Lotus Consulting & Marketing LLC, where she helps organizations and individuals align strategy, vision, and purpose.

From conference stages to community gatherings, Tamiko shares practical wisdom on resilience, leadership, and personal branding, leaving audiences encouraged and empowered.

Grief, Giggles & Grace is her debut book, born from the deeply personal journey of losing her mother. Through humor, faith, and storytelling, she offers comfort and light to those navigating the path of grief.

Tamiko makes her home in Atlanta, Georgia, where she finds joy in sharing tea with friends, creating safe spaces for laughter and healing, and honoring her mother's legacy by living boldly.

LET'S CONTINUE THE JOURNEY

Beyond these pages, I'm here—writing, speaking, and helping people navigate transitions, lead with confidence, and build meaningful brands.

Connect with me:
▶ **@TamikoDrummondAuthor** on Instagram
For updates on upcoming books, speaking engagements, leadership insights, and fresh perspectives on resilience and growth.

Join the Grief, Giggles & Grace community:
▶ **@griefgigglesgrace** on Instagram
For daily encouragement, scripture, and connection with others on the healing path.

▶**www.GriefGiggleAndGrace.com**

Your story is still unfolding. Let's walk forward together.

REFERENCES & RESOURCES

Books Cited & Recommended

Devine, Megan. *It's OK That You're Not OK: Meeting Grief and Loss in a Culture That Doesn't Understand.* Sounds True, 2017.

O'Connor, Mary-Frances. *The Grieving Brain: The Surprising Science of How We Learn from Love and Loss.* HarperOne, 2022.

Podcasts

Lloyd, Cariad. *Griefcast.* Available at: griefcast.com

Terrible, Thanks for Asking. APM Studios. Available at: ttfa.org

Scripture References

Scripture quotations marked (NIV) are taken from the Holy Bible, New International Version®, NIV®. Copyright © 1973, 1978, 1984, 2011 by Biblica, Inc.® Used by permission. All rights reserved worldwide.

Scripture quotations marked (NLT) are taken from the Holy Bible, New Living Translation, copyright © 1996, 2004, 2015 by Tyndale House Foundation. Used by permission of Tyndale House Publishers, Inc., Carol Stream, Illinois 60188. All rights reserved.

Scripture quotations marked (KJV) are taken from the King James Version of the Bible, which is in the public domain.

Additional Support Resources

If you are experiencing grief and need additional support, please consider:

- **National Alliance for Grieving Children:** nacg.org
- **The Dinner Party:** thedinnerparty.org (grief support for 21-45s)
- **GriefShare:** griefshare.org (faith-based grief support groups)